Dear Al & Ernie
        I pray that this
bring you peace comfort & joy. God bless You.

Love you

Lucy

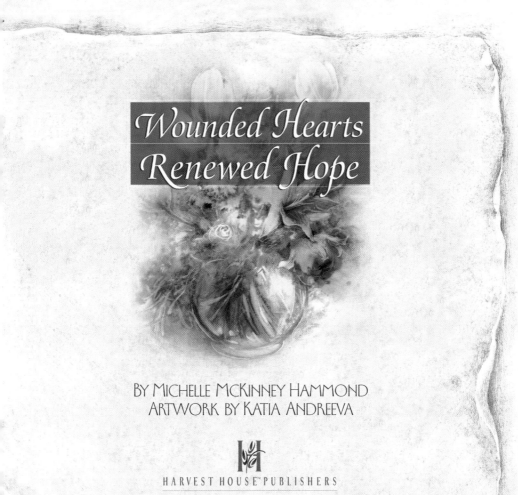

Wounded Hearts
Renewed Hope

By Michelle McKinney Hammond
Artwork by Katia Andreeva

HARVEST HOUSE PUBLISHERS

EUGENE, OREGON

Wounded Hearts—Renewed Hope

Text Copyright © 2002 Michelle McKinney Hammond
Artwork Copyright © 2002 Katia Andreeva
Published by Harvest House Publishers
Eugene, Oregon 97402

Published in association with the literary agency of Alive Communications, Inc.,
7680 Goddard Street, Suite 200, Colorado Springs, CO 80920

McKinney Hammond, Michelle, 1957-
  Wounded hearts—renewed hope / by Michelle McKinney Hammond ; artwork by Katia Andreeva.
    p. cm. — (Matters of the heart series)
  ISBN 0-7369-0978-8 (Hardcover : alk. paper)
  1. Single women—Prayer-books and devotions—English. 2. Single women—Religious life. I. Title. II. Series.
BV4596.S5 M352 2002
242'.6432—dc21   2002002160

Other Books by Michelle McKinney Hammond

Intimate Thoughts, Whispered Prayers
What to Do Until Love Finds You
Secrets of an Irresistible Woman
Where Are You, God?
The Power of Femininity
Get a Love Life
If Men Are Like Buses Then How Do I Catch One?
Prayer Guide for the Brokenhearted
What Becomes of the Brokenhearted
How to Be Blessed and Highly Favored

To correspond with Ms. McKinney Hammond, write to: HeartWing Ministries, P.O. Box 11052, Chicago, IL
60611; or email her at heartwingmin@yahoo.com. For speaking engagement inquiries contact: Speak Up
Speaker Services, 1-888-870-7719.

Design and production by Koechel Peterson and Associates, Minneapolis, Minnesota

Scripture quotations are from the Holy Bible, New International Version®, Copyright © 1973, 1978, 1984 by
the International Bible Society. Used by permission of Zondervan Publishing House.

Printed in Hong Kong.

02 03 04 05 06 07 08 09 10 11 / NG/ 10 9 8 7 6 5 4 3 2 1

Here's to all those who have

had tearstained pillows,

sighed wordless prayers,

dried the tears of others while fighting their own,

fought their way back from the pit of despair

and those still wandering through the valley...

Keep the faith...

God is there

even when your tears blur your view.

*Barbara, Shana, Katia, I think four are better than one! Thank
you for making everything I write ring true so beautifully. To my
Harvest House family, I'm so glad I have a home with you.*

Dear Wounded Heart

I feel your pain...

And though my situation might not have been yours exactly,

I have been assaulted by the same shock. The same anger.

The same depression. I have struggled with unforgiveness—

the inability to let go. I, too, have wondered if I will ever

recover—ever trust again, begin again, and be able to

move on. Yes, I have been there. But thanks to the grace

of God, I am no longer there.

This is my offering of hope to you. I am a

living witness to the fact that God is able.

Not only to comfort you, but to bring

you through your present brokenness. It doesn't stop there. He will take the broken pieces of your heart and fashion them into an incredible vessel of priceless value. He will rebuild your spirit and make you whole again. More beautiful than before, transforming every scar into a beauty mark that others admire.

So dare to hope...and believe that the Son will shine again. Walk the path slowly, one step at a time, until you reach your destination...the land of healing and wholeness.

Michelle

YESTERDAY

Yesterday

I cried more than a river

I let loose

an ocean

a universe of tears

and then some

Weeping for more than a night

I thought I would drown in my pain

But then You came

promising to exchange my ocean

for Your rain

soft and warm

rinsing away my yesterdays

giving me hope for yet another day...

Rinsin

Dear Heavenly Father,

I know that You have promised to dry every tear, but sometimes I feel as if I will never stop weeping. I long for the joy You promise in the morning but I feel lost in the night. I am in desperate need of Your comfort, Your touch. A reason for going on. Please speak to the storm in my life and let Your peace surround me. Cause my lamentation to cease with Your sweet promises and hold me close until the pain passes over, in Jesus' Name, I pray. *Amen.*

Sometimes I hope

Sometimes I wonder

sometimes I hope

sometimes I merely exist

convinced of no better tomorrow

I am bound to the memories of better days now gone by

unable to imagine restoration

Though I know tomorrow is not based on what I see

still I find no more light

than where I stand for now

and I cannot move forward

therefore I must look up instead...

Dear God,

I know that You know the plans You have for me, but I don't. The darkness of my trial has made it hard for me to see. I am lost in the darkness, overwhelmed with my pain, and yet I have a remembrance of Your goodness as I await Your visitation. Perhaps I have been too absorbed within myself to look up and be found in You. For this I ask forgiveness and ask for Your strength to help me hope again, in Jesus' Name. *Amen.*

words for life

Betrayed by life

that's how I felt

as if a friend had grabbed my throat

and choked the very joy out of my being

and all that is left is the unbelief

that such a thing could happen

The helplessness of others to fix the unfixable

only deepens my despair

And yet I recall Your promise

You will not leave me comfortless...

I cling to those words for life...

Your promise

Dear Heavenly Father,

You are the only One

who can reach the place that hurts within me. Even I cannot put my finger on the exact place for I am consumed by my pain. Disappointment, anger, frustration...are just a few of the feelings that swirl within, leaving me feeling drained. I find myself unable to say much more than help me, in Jesus' Name. *Amen.*

come alive

If this is what shock gives way to

then truly numbness is bliss

For now that the nerve endings of my emotions

have come alive

this new fury I feel

frightens me...

I don't know how to put out the fire

nor chart its direction...

It spreads to the left
to the right

its flames even leaping toward heaven

And I am helpless to put it out

before the sun goes down on my wrath

I pray for tears to quench its destructive determination

and You send Your rain where my tears can't reach

to rinse my pain

and quiet the storm within me...

Dear Heavenly Father,

I must admit that I am angry.

Angry because I hurt. Angry that You have allowed me to experience this pain. I am just angry. I don't really know where to direct it or how to curb it. I want to lash out, but where? And would that satisfy my pain or cause me more in the long run? I need You to quench the flames in my heart that threaten to consume me. Quiet my spirit and grant me peace. Help me to release all that I cannot control and trust You, in Jesus' Name I pray. *Amen.*

to imagine

Dare I talk about it one more time?

As if rehearsing every little detail

could erase the present facts

And yet it seems irresistible

the pull to recall

to remember

to imagine what would be if things were different

And yet they are not

They are exactly what they are

Sad but true

the reality bites me

my spirit feels the sting

Yet deep within I feel another sensation

Your soothing touch

nudging me to move forward...

soothin

Dear God,

I don't like what has happened in my life. It is hard for me to know where to go from here. I find myself clinging to yesterday simply because I know no more than where I've already been. I am frightened. Afraid of what that means for tomorrow. I find myself fighting doubt. What else will You allow? Recovery seems to be a distant hope. Bring me closer to the reality of being whole again, in Jesus' Name. *Amen.*

Cover Me

Cover me...

Cover me with Your spirit

like a mother covers her child with a comforter

and let me lose myself beneath its folds...

staying beneath the warmth of it

For right now the world feels too cold

If I could hide forever I would

but I know that while You promise joy in the morning

I am still waiting for it

as I sink deeper beneath my despair

Sometimes sneaking a quick check

on life's temperature

I find it is still winter

I weep

I cry

I long for spring...

prom

Dear Father,

I am speechless.

Bound in my pain. I have exhausted myself and find that I am unable to unwrap myself from my depression. I long for the light and yet I find it hurts my eyes. And I draw back from the joy You offer because on one hand it feels better to embrace my grief. Perhaps I am afraid of what grasping joy will mean. Finality. Acknowledging that it is over. I don't know if I'm ready for that, and yet I am. Help me win the fight, O God, in Jesus' Name. *Amen.*

Trusting You

Somewhere in the back of my spirit
I sense a light at the end of my struggle
I walk toward it hesitantly
unsure of where it leads
yet desiring a new place I move on
Two steps forward
Three steps back
I cringe before my feet land
afraid of where I'll find myself
I struggle with trusting You
yet having no choice
I will move or die
Die or die trying
Which one appeals to me more
I haven't decided
Perhaps knowing that You will never leave me
or forsake me is enough for now
Enough to keep me reaching toward You...

sens

Dear Heavenly Father,

Help me, I am paralyzed

I want to move on but find that I am hopelessly stuck in the regrets of yesterday. I admit that I also struggle with trusting You. If You allowed this to happen, will You allow me to be hurt and disappointed again? The thought is more than I can bear. And yet You promise to be near to me. I need to feel Your nearness and be reassured of Your goodness. Take my hand, precious Lord, lead me from this place and restore my hope, in Jesus' Name. *Amen.*

Promises

All things work to the good You say...

Promises, promises

Weeping may endure for a night

but joy comes in the morning...

Promises, promises

Many are the afflictions of the righteous

but the Lord delivers us out of them all...

Promises, promises

No weapon the enemy has designed against me

will accomplish its mission

Promises, promises...

Precious promises

I cling to

and breathlessly repeat...

Lord, help my unbelief...

Dear Heavenly Father,

This situation has shattered my faith. Perhaps that is my fault because I misplaced my trust. You are the only one that is true and faithful, consistent, trustworthy and most of all eternal. As You nurse my wounds, also nurse my faith. Renew my hope. Whisper words of comfort. Remind me of Your promises which are always *yea* and *amen.* I am comforted by the fact that You cannot lie. Repeat Your promises to me again and let them be anchored in my soul, in Jesus' Name.

Amen.

Turn to You

I don't understand what

I don't understand why

Still I will turn to You...

I don't understand how

I don't know when You will come for me

still I will wait for You

I cannot weep

I cannot pray

I cannot fight

I cannot face another day

but still I will believe in You

Still I will cling to Your word

Still I will accept what I cannot see

or comprehend

Against all hope

I will hope in You

Still...

Hope

Why are you downcast, O my soul?
Why so disturbed within me? Put your hope in God,
for I will yet praise him, my Savior and my God.

—Psalm 42:5

TODAY

The sun came out today

and for a moment

I could see tomorrow clearly

But then clouds came threatening

to rain on my happiness once again

And I shivered in the sudden cool breeze

of the realization

that nothing was different

Nothing had changed

Including the fact that You are faithful

No matter what...

Faithful

Dear Heavenly Father,

Though I know it takes time to heal I find myself growing impatient with my pain. Please continue to wash my wounds and strengthen me. Help me to let go of yesterday and dare to hope again. Open my eyes to see my tomorrows as You see them. And help me to trust Your heart even when I don't see what You hold in Your hands, simply because You've promised that it is all good, in Jesus' Name. *Amen.*

Expectations

Today
I worried about tomorrow
though there was nothing I could do about it
I tried to shape
its invisible folds into
something I could try on
but my expectations slipped through my hands
and crumbled to fine dust that I could not
recover...
And my only present accomplishment
was to learn that
sufficient are the trials of the day
better left until they've had their say...

trials of the day

Lord,

Help me to relax

and not run ahead of You. Help me to concentrate on the lessons at hand, the healing that is available right here, right now. Don't let me become distracted by things I can do nothing about. Help me to stay focused on You, receiving my daily bread and being nourished back to health today. And based on the knowledge that You are the great "I Am," help me to live in the present, in Jesus' Name. *Amen.*

Small Blossom

While searching among the weeds of my pain

I found a blossom

Small and shy

Hidden from the light

But beautiful just the same

One small blossom

Promising more in due time

Lifting its face toward the Son

Bursting with hope

Anticipating better tomorrows

Where joy could flourish once again...

Promising

Dear Lord,

Help me to cling
to the rays of light and hope that You give.
Strengthen me to rise above my depression and
embrace Your joy. You have promised to turn my
mourning into dancing. I am awaiting Your music. I
long to be caught up in Your rhythm and reverber-
ate with Your praise. Play the strings of my heart
and make me an instrument of worship to the praise
of Your glorious goodness, in Jesus' Name. *Amen.*

Clouds flee

Shadows race across my spirit
beginning to dissipate
The Son is rising....
Clouds flee
rains cease
a rainbow forms
reminding me of Your faithful promises

Joy is coming
round the bend slowly
more slowly than I would like
but surely
I'm beginning to see the light...

Oh Heavenly Father,

Thank You.

Even when I was faithless You remained faithful. Forgive me for the times I wondered if I would ever experience joy again. In spite of what You promised, I wavered. Thank You for Your determination to help me embrace what I fail to see at times. I realize that this is just the beginning, help me to take it one day at a time, in Jesus' Name. *Amen.*

emotion

One day at a time
>> brick by brick

One step at a time
>> I will rebuild my shattered remains

Moment by moment
>> I will see them rise

Emotion upon emotion
>> I see them taking familiar shape

Mood upon mood
>> the same but different

Sometimes up
Sometimes down
>> I keep moving onward and upward
>> knowing I will reach my destination of wholeness
>> if I don't faint...

The mountain looms in sight
I prepare myself for the climb
>> and I keep my eyes focused on the top of the pinnacle
>> I plan to crown....

Dear Heavenly Father,

Help me not to grow weary

as I walk toward my healing. Or grow impatient with myself when I experience setbacks. Help me to trust You one day at a time, not trying to run ahead to solidify my future. Give me my daily bread, and I will rest in You and let You hold my tomorrows. In Jesus' Name. *Amen.*

Laugh out loud

I laughed out loud today
and it was music to my ears
Like the early morning song
of birds in flight
refreshed from a night's rest
I felt my spirit take flight
lighter than it has been for a time
and I enjoyed the freedom of flying
above my circumstances
Higher, higher
my problems looking
smaller, smaller
My faith carrying my heart
to another place where I sense new life springing
from old weary places...
Such is life from another point of view
I could grow used to rising above my pain...

Dear Heavenly Father,

Thank You, thank You, thank You!

Thank You for the gift of laughter. The gift of being able to see light at the end of the tunnel. Thank You for guiding me there. I am so grateful that You are close to the brokenhearted. Truly it is by Your grace that I've made it this far. Continue to hold my hand and lead me back to the place of consistent joy, in Jesus' Name. *Amen.*

Whispered

Looking in the mirror

I see a face
seasoned by time

and lessons learned

Some needing to be repeated

but passing the test

I am older and wiser for my misfortune...

Pain whispered some things

shouted others

and I have listened
Listened and comprehended

Now armed with understanding, I move on...

toward a better day

**in which I am better for the
tears and trials**

Better for the knowing

it doesn't end here...

Dear Heavenly Father,

I never thought I would say it
but I am a better person because of what I have been
through. And You in Your omniscience knew that all
along. Truly all things do work together for the
good. I am now a witness. Still some days are better
than others but I have learned to embrace my pain
and learn from it. Thank You for the lessons. Thank
You for helping me pass the tests, in Jesus' Name.
Amen.

fresh and new

I recognized the pain in her eyes

I had been there

I recalled the feelings

And for a moment they washed over me

just as fresh and new

as when first felt

And I longed to reach out to her

to offer a comforting word

to share that life would go on

that she would live and laugh again...

These were facts that I now

intimately knew...

And so the circle of life continues

The reward being that pain is useful

for healing others...

Dear Lord,

You were wounded for my sake and acquainted with grief in order to not only pay the price for my salvation, but to sympathize with my every need. You have called us to comfort others with comfort that You have given us. Though I am healed and whole, never let me forget the lesson learned in my brokenness. Let me use them to bless others who are hurting. Give me a heart of empathy to help others find the path to healing, in Jesus' Name. *Amen.*

greater grace

Inhale

Exhale

It feels good to breathe again

a fresh new wind

to be intoxicated with His spirit

filling me with greater hope

deeper understanding

greater grace

more insight into His constant mercy...

It's clearer now

sweeter

far more precious than before

And I am in awe of the beauty of being broken

blessed and restored

to live in a greater light...

More precious

Dear Heavenly Father,

Just as You breathed the breath of life into the original man, breathe again into me...refreshing my inner being. And even as Your words of comfort wash over me and Your spirit refills me, grant me complete renewal of heart, soul, mind, and strength that I might run and not grow weary, walk and not faint. May I never tire of well doing, knowing that You will always be my great reward, in Jesus' Name. *Amen.*

Fresh thoughts

Fresh thoughts
and wishes for new direction
have all led me to this place
never visited

Awaiting my exploration
new footprints in the sand
original in nature
leaving new impressions...

The joy of new mercies
and beginning again...

See, I am doing a new thing! Now it springs up;
do you not perceive it? I am making a way
in the desert and streams in the wasteland.

—Isaiah 43:19

TOMORROW

The sun rose today

inside of me and out my window

promising spring

and warmth on the horizon

New feelings

new faith

new mercies

new strength

to go the distance

and finish the journey

And for the first time it's clear to me

that I'm going somewhere

And my heart is finally willing to follow

trusting in a brighter tomorrow...

the journey

Dear Heavenly Father,

Thank You for carrying me

when I didn't have the strength to walk. For drying my tears when I feared that I was drowning in them. Thank You for being faithful while I was yet faithless. For speaking peace to the tempest in me. Teaching me to walk on water. Showing me that I could indeed make it to the other side. And now I pray: Lead me toward that which You've so carefully planned for me, in Jesus' Name. *Amen.*

my emotions

Promises of things to come

fill my spirit

with heaven's rhythms

pounding in harmony with my heart

putting a bounce in my step

lifting my soul off the ground

teaching me to fly

above my emotions

and questions

with reckless abandon

apart from all I've known

and experienced

I trust

I believe,

the best is yet to come...

Dear Lord,

My heart is full with expectancy. Like a woman carrying the precious seed of life yet to come, my cup runneth over with anticipation of Your restoration and blessing untold. Prepare me to embrace the new season of my life that You have planned. Help me not to look back but to press on and take hold of the prize that awaits me. And let my testimony be one that spreads the news of Your goodness abroad to many, in Jesus' Name. *Amen.*

spectacular

New every morning

mercies unfold

Things not expected yesterday

only revealing themselves

in the morrow

Fresh manna

not to be collected and stored

but discovered with each spectacular dawning

challenging me to take one day at a time

watching the hand of God unfold

to present new treasures

that keep me moving toward His throne

spurred on by the curiosity

of seeing what

each new day will bring...

new tre

Dear Heavenly Father,

You have said not to fret about tomorrow for sufficient is the trouble of each new day. But I would like to add to that. Overwhelming are the blessings of each new day. I see the glass half full now instead of half empty, steadily getting fuller. I see a new side of You. The side I could not see before, so distracted was I by my present. But You have shown me that You go before me with greater plans than I had ever dreamed, leaving me speechless in my adoration of You. Show me what I can render unto You in exchange for all You've done, in Jesus' Name. *Amen.*

my breath

Just when I thought I had caught my breath

You take it away again

replacing it with something sweeter

far more profound and true

Exchanging evil for good

making me fruitful

in the land of my affliction

Presenting me with succulent fare

truly worth the agony of the pruning

preparing the ground of my spirit to yield

even more

And I am made a living witness

to the mysteries of Your heart...

Your heart

Dear Heavenly Father,

Why do we constantly try to second guess You? Your ways are past finding out until You decide to reveal Your hand. I am grieved over the times that I failed to trust You. I find myself embarrassed by these new blessings. Things I had no faith for. Yet in spite of me, You move on my behalf. Who am I that You are mindful of me in my broken state? Should I ever pass this way again, help me to remember the lessons learned and stay true to them, in Jesus' Name. *Amen.*

the blessings

Tomorrow asks me questions

that I cannot answer

and I no longer despair of this

Like the night before Christmas

gazing at unfamiliar shapes

under the tree

I now consider the blessings

wrapped at the foot of the cross

daily awaiting my unwrapping

in exchange for the burdens

that I leave there

tentatively letting go of what I know

to embrace all that's yet to be unearthed...

daily

Dear Heavenly Father,

Please forgive

my suspicious nature. My insistence of knowing everything before the fact. Though You've proven Yourself time and time again, I find myself still taking baby steps toward You. Wobbling, sometimes falling as I stagger at the prospect of trusting You completely. And yet You hold out Your arms and wait for me. Wait for me to run to You with no other thought in mind, but reaching Your throne. Strengthen my trust for the journey, in Jesus' Name.

Amen.

Your goodness

A crowd of witnesses
urge me onward
telling me of Your goodness
and miracles past
Those that I have been privy to
and those unknown
They urge me toward the finish line
with smiles on their faces
reassuring me that it was all worth it
the pain
the not knowing
but most of all
the things that were left behind
in order to make room for the greater...

Rea

Dear Lord,

It is hard to perceive of or even comprehend the new thing that You are doing in my life. And yet hints of wonderfulness arrest my fears and my tendency to draw back. You have whet my appetite. Seduced my curious nature and my desire to be whole. And so, in spite of all that I do not know, I pursue You, refusing to let You go until You show me all that You hold in Your hands. Now that I am fully aware of Your presence, show me Your glory, in Jesus' Name. *Amen.*

more fulfillment

From the place of weeping

　　to dreaming

　　　to greater darkness still

to unexpected light

　　to waiting in vain

　or seemingly so

　to the place of more fulfillment

　　than one soul can hold

　　　You take me from glory to glory

never seeming to exhaust

　　Your store...

　and I dare not think of the future

　for long moments of time

　　so overwhelmed am I

　　　at Your goodness in the present...

Dear Omniscient Father,

I am so glad

that You know all things. So finite is my understanding that I would only limit myself and Your potential if You were held captive within my imagination. So much greater than the box I put You in, You continue to prove Yourself when there is nothing else to prove. Let each revelation of Your infinite grace and blessing be a stepping-stone to greater faith in You, in Jesus' Name. *Amen.*

Grace

Grace...

is so much more

than something said before a meal

infinitely greater

it speaks before each blessing

heralding Your arrival

in my situation

Turning the tide

breaking the rules

my expectations

You continue to surprise me

when You should no longer

For whenever I settle into my understanding of You

as I know it

You do a new thing

breaking another rule

and say grace all over again...

Dear Heavenly Father,

I know that it is by Your grace alone that I am standing here. Whole again. Though the traces of my brokenness remain to remind me of where You've brought me from, I find the outlines of what You put back together again beautiful. They reflect the character of a beautiful vessel tried by fire in the hands of a Master craftsman. And I am humbled by the knowledge that I am Your personal work of art. Let me bring You glory and be a credit to Your workmanship, in Jesus' Name. *Amen.*

moving forward

Turning the corner

never to turn around

moving forward

never going back

A new chapter

a new day

new mercies I see

the old has passed away

leaving only lessons learned

wisdom replacing naiveté

experience doing its work

making me stronger than before

and finally I am able to find the diamonds

in all of my tears...

new day

Dear Heavenly Father,

Thank You for new beginnings. Just when I think You can do nothing greater than what You have already done, You outdo Yourself. Ever unfolding. Taking me to higher heights in You, taking me above my circumstances. Offering me a bird's-eye view of life. Revealing to me the big picture. I am astounded that life doesn't end at my troubles. It is only the beginning of a greater revelation of Your grace. Continue to show me more, in Jesus' Name. *Amen.*

Today is now

Yesterday

was then what it was

Today is now
the ever present

quickly turning into tomorrow

which is yet to come bearing its own treasures

and surprises

defeats and victories

all taken in stride

because I know the One

who has written all my days

In this I rest assured,

that all of my days are ordered

and my happy ending is ensured...

I rest

Dear Heavenly Father,

It's good to know that I can rest in the plans You have for me. Plans of *yea* and *amen*. Good versus evil, hope instead of hopelessness. A future of eternal joy, peace, and fulfillment. You have promised to collect all my tears and present them to me. Washing me in the newness of life and eternal security. Thank You for keeping me ever in Your care, in the center of Your divine plan even when I can't see my way. Continue to lead me Lord—through it all, lead me to Your arms, in Jesus' Name. *Amen.*

My Covenant

I now renew my covenant with You.

To trust You in spite of my circumstances. To know that You are working all things for good to my ultimate fulfillment and the praise of Your glory. I pledge to be a living witness, giving testimony of Your faithfulness to all those around me—to comfort those with the comfort You have given me. This is my promise to You.

> *From my heart*
> *to Your throne*
> *in this moment and*
> *for all my tomorrows.*

_____
(your signature here)

_____
(date)

You turned my wailing into dancing; You removed my sackcloth and clothed me with joy, that my heart may sing to You and not be silent. O LORD my God, I will give You thanks forever.

–PSALM 30:11-12